Relationships and Finances

Finances

Managing Money Matters Together

Table of Contents

Chapter 1. Introduction

Welcome to the engaging and essential world of "Relationships and Finances: Managing Money Matters Together". This isn't just a Special Report; consider it your guide to creating financial harmony in your love life. Navigating finances as a team is no easy feat, but hold your trepidations at bay, as our expert recommendations, tips, and strategies can turn this daunting endeavor into a journey of growth, connection, and empowerment. Be it budgeting basics, joint investments, or sensible spending, we leave no stone unturned. Prepare to embark on this enlightening journey that promises to balance both your checkbook and love life, transforming financial talks from stressful to celebratory. Embrace the opportunity to strengthen your relationship through the shared understanding of finance – after reading this report, you'll wonder why money talks were ever a point of contention in the first place!

Chapter 2. Setting Shared Financial Goals

Setting shared financial goals as a couple is a multi-step process requiring both parties to engage in open dialogues, reach consensus, plan, track, and eventually achieve those goals. Through collective decision-making, couples not only reinforce their commitment towards each other but also lay the foundation for a secure financial future.

2.1. Importance of Setting Shared Financial Goals

Imagine sailing a ship without a destination. It's quite a fruitless endeavor, isn't it? In a similar vein, having distinct financial goals can be the North Star in your journey towards achieving monetary prosperity and economic stability as a couple. Not only does it help you align your money habits and expectations but also strengthens your bond as you work together to make these dreams a reality. A well-constructed financial goal provides a clear vision, eliminates unnecessary expenditures, and instills a disciplined savings habit, improving the overall financial health and economic well-being of the couple.

2.2. Initiating Conversations about Money

One of the first steps towards setting shared financial goals is initiating conversations about money. Though discussing money matters might be uncomfortable, approach the situation as a team with understanding, patience, and a no-judgment policy. Start with sharing your individual perspectives on money and finance, your upbringing, and how it has shaped your current financial behavior. Understand each other's financial standing, values, aspirations, debts, savings, and income sources. Embrace transparency because a clear, honest financial picture is fundamental to setting shared financial goals.

2.3. Identifying and Discussing Your Financial Goals

After gaining a solid understanding of each other's financial perspectives, the next step would be to identify and discuss what your financial aspirations and goals look like. These could range from short-term goals like paying off credit card debt or saving for vacation, to long-term goals such as retirement savings, owning a house, or funding your children's education. Prioritize these goals based on urgency, importance, and feasibility. Understand that, just like your preferences and personalities, your financial goals can also differ and that's perfectly okay. What's important is finding a compromise or a joint goal that both of you can agree on.

2.4. Setting S.M.A.R.T Goals

When setting financial goals as a couple, it's beneficial to have S.M.A.R.T. goals - these are Specific, Measurable, Attainable, Relevant, and Time-bound. For instance, your goal could be to 'Save $10,000 for a down payment on a house in 2 years'. This goal is specific ($10,000), measurable (by tracking savings), attainable (depending on your combined income), relevant (the home goal previously discussed), and time-bound (2 years). By setting S.M.A.R.T goals, you are guiding your money towards a well-defined path with clear expectations.

2.5. Developing a Strategic Plan

Once your goals are set, the next step is to create a strategic plan to achieve them. This could involve creating a joint budget, having a savings plan, cutting down on unnecessary expenses, and finding additional income sources. Brainstorm together and utilize budgeting tools or apps, financial planners, or consultants if required. Make sure to revisit and readjust this plan based on changes in income, expenses, market conditions, personal circumstances, or objectives.

2.6. Communication and Regular Check-ins

Ensure that you keep the lines of communication open at all times. Money matters and financial goals are not a one-time conversation. They need regular check-ins, discussions, and yearly financial reviews. Celebrate small wins, and remember, setbacks are just opportunities for reassessment and realignment.

2.7. Respecting Individual Financial Autonomy

Despite having shared goals and pooling resources, it's essential to respect each other's financial autonomy. Allow space for personal discretionary spending without guilt or judgment. Just because you're a team does not mean you have to lose your individuality.

2.8. Seeking Professional Help

Lastly, don't shy away from seeking professional help if required. A financial adviser with experience in working with couples can provide invaluable advice, mediate discussions, and guide your financial decisions towards achieving your shared financial goals.

In conclusion, shared financial goals form a critical component of any successful relationship. They foster mutual understanding, respect, collaboration, and create a road map towards financial security. Remember, in this journey of joint financial planning, the discourse does not end with achieving a set goal, rather, it involves continuous engagement, evaluation, and recalibration to ensure lasting financial harmony.

Chapter 3. Sensible Spending: Deciphering Needs vs Wants

Defining expenditure as essential or discretionary is an integral part of any financial planning. But more often than not, these lines blur. Managing money efficiently is about making sure we spend on our needs and are judicious about our wants. That's exactly where 'Sensible Spending' steps in.

3.1. The Essentiality of Sensible Spending

Sensible spending is a financial behavior that encourages judicious use of your earned money. It deters impulsive purchases and promotes deliberate, necessity-based buying decisions. The concept is simple to understand but often challenging to implement due to the ubiquity of consumer culture, advertisements, and the human tendency to seek instant gratification.

By adopting sensible spending habits, you can ensure that the lion's share of your finances goes towards securing your needs, creating a financial buffer, and aligning with your long-term financial goals. Ideally, discretionary spending or wants should not impede these crucial areas.

3.2. Need vs Want: Understanding the Difference

Before cultivating sensible spending habits, it's crucial to clearly distinguish between your needs and your wants.

A 'need' is something you require for survival or general functioning

- food, shelter, healthcare, basic clothing, etc. In other words, these expenses are non-negotiable.

On the other hand, a 'want' denotes commodities or experiences considered extras or luxuries. These vary immensely from individual to individual and can include anything from a high-end smartphone to a fancy vacation.

The line between needs and wants often gets blurred. For instance, while having a phone might be a need, owning the latest iPhone model is a want. Herein lies one of the significant challenges of sensible spending: neutralizing our desire for non-essentials and focusing more on necessities.

3.3. Practical Strategies for Sensible Spending

The journey to sensible spending starts with self-awareness and taking actionable steps consciously. Here are a few practical strategies you can consider:

Creating a Budget: The first and the most crucial step towards sensible spending is creating a comprehensive, realistic budget. List down all your expenses and categorize them into needs and wants. By visualizing your spending habits, you can identify areas of unnecessary expenditure and curb them.

Implementing the 50-30-20 rule: This is a popular budgeting technique, where 50% of your income goes to needs, 30% to wants, and 20% towards savings or paying off debt. This rule provides a clear guideline on how to allocate your income.

Setting Financial Goals: Having short-term and long-term financial goals can steer your spending behavior. Whenever you're tempted to indulge in a 'want', remind yourself of your goals.

Practicing Delayed Gratification: Instead of making impulsive purchases, practice waiting for a few days before buying a want. This delay can help curtail unnecessary spending.

3.4. Inculcating Sensible Spending in Your Relationship

Managing finances as a couple can be challenging, but it also opens up opportunities for meaningful conversations and shared decision-making. Here are a few steps to encourage sensible spending within your relationship:

Discuss Financial Goals: Regularly discuss your financial goals as a couple. Have long-term goals such as retirement plans, buying a house, or travel plans, and short-term goals like saving for a fancy date or a weekend getaway. This not only fosters financial communication but aligns your spending habits with common goals.

Plan a Joint Budget: Planning a budget together creates financial transparency, instills a sense of shared responsibility, and encourages a cooperative approach to spending patterns.

Celebrate Milestones: Whenever you achieve a savings milestone or successfully adhere to your budget for a certain period, celebrate together. This reinforces positive spending behaviors and deepens your bond.

3.5. Sensible Spending: A Key to Financial Harmony

Practicing sensible spending won't just impact your financial health; it will also enhance mutual understanding, trust, and cooperation in your relationship. With consistent practice, patience, and perseverance, you can Foster a healthy financial environment where money is no longer a source of contention, but a tool for advancing shared dreams and aspirations. The journey might require adjustments, trade-offs, and renegotiating wants. But in the end, the sense of financial security, harmony, and shared accomplishment is genuinely worth it.

Sensible spending is not about completely eliminating wants; rather, it's about achieving a balance where needs are prioritized, and wants are fulfilled judiciously. Here's to a journey of financial awareness, responsible spending, and mutual growth! Try these tips and incorporate them into your life. Enjoy the simple pleasures that sensible spending brings - peace of mind, stronger relationships, a secure future, and the freedom to spend on meaningful experiences and things you genuinely value.

After all, mastering money and relationships isn't just about numbers; it's about understanding your spending behaviors, making conscious choices, aligning your financial actions with your life goals, and creating a shared vision of prosperity with your partner. This journey of money management is indeed an expedition filled with learnings, realizations, and triumphs! Happy mindful spending!

Chapter 4. Budgeting Basics for Couples

Knowing where your money goes and how much you have to save or spend is critical for setting financial goals. Whether you're saving for a vacation, a new car, or a nest egg, good budgeting habits can help you reach those goals. A budget doesn't limit your freedom - it gives you freedom by setting clear boundaries and helping you build a safety net.

4.1. Understanding Each Other's Financial History

While it's crucial to discuss future financial goals as a couple, understanding each other's financial pasts is just as important. This involves discussing your spending habits, attitudes towards money, and financial issues that you've each encountered in the past. Reflect on prior experiences and determine together what changes could be implemented to improve your joint approach to finances.

Take time to discuss:

- How much debt you both are carrying and how you are planning to pay it off.

- What your savings goals are and what the funds will be used for.

- How much income you each bring in, along with any potential for income growth.

- Whether you have a good credit score and, if not, what steps you can take to improve it.

- Whether you'll maintain separate, combined, or a mix of both types of accounts.

This initial conversation can help lay a foundation for your shared financial approach.

4.2. Implementing a Joint Budget

Once you've decided how your finances will be arranged, it's time to create your budget. A budget is a summary of estimated income and expenses for a given period. It helps you spend within your means and reach financial goals.

Start by tracking your income and expenses for a month or two to get a sense of where the money comes from and where it goes. Record everything, from major monthly payments like rent and car payments, to smaller incidental expenses like coffee runs and grocery bills.

With this detailed understanding, allot categories for essential expenses such as bills, groceries, and rent or mortgage. Deduct these from your total joint income. The remaining money can be divided between optional expenses and savings. While optional expenses can be anything from gym memberships to leisure activities, ensure a proportionate amount (a recommended 20% of your income) goes into your savings or emergency fund.

4.3. Using Tools for Tracking and Organizing

In the modern digital age, numerous finance and budgeting apps make the process of tracking expenses and organizing budgets convenient. Money management apps like Mint, You Need a Budget (YNAB), and PocketGuard are fantastic tools to visualize your spending habits, set savings goals, and see your financial progress in real-time.

If you prefer something more traditional, a simple spreadsheet or even a pen-and-paper ledger can effectively keep track of your income and expenses. Whatever tool you choose should suit both partners' preferences and habits. They should be easy to understand and update regularly.

4.4. Regular Financial Review Meetings

Creating a budget is only the first step. To stay on track, it's key to regularly review your budget. Schedule monthly or bi-monthly 'finance date nights' where you go over your budget, check in on your financial goals, see where you've made progress, and discuss areas that need adjustment.

It is not unusual for expenses to fluctuate month to month, with some unexpected costs cropping up occasionally. Do check the budget vs actual spend data. If you're repeatedly going over-budget in a particular category, it might be time to reassess and adjust the allocations.

These meetings are not intended to point fingers but to provide transparency and a joint effort to reach your financial goals.

4.5. Planning for Emergencies

Even with the best-laid plans, life can throw curveballs. This could be in the form of a sudden break down of your car or an unexpected medical issue or a sudden job loss. It's essential to account for such contingencies.

Financial advisors recommend setting aside three to six months' worth of living expenses in an emergency fund. By doing this, unexpected costs can be mitigated without derailing overall financial health or goals.

4.6. Conclusion

While managing finances as a couple can be challenging, having a shared understanding of where the money goes, setting mutual financial goals, and effectively communicating your needs and expectations can alleviate a lot of potential stress. By following these practical steps and establishing a shared approach to budgeting, you can create a solid plan towards reaching your financial goals together. Remember: transparency, support, and empathy are critical components to financial success as a couple.

Chapter 5. Dealing with Debt: The Duo's Guide

Debt is rarely a subject that couples address with smiles. Yet, navigating this challenging terrain together can be tremendously rewarding. According to the American Psychological Association, approximately 72% of Americans reported feeling stressed about money at least some of the time during the past month.

Through combined efforts, debts can become manageable, if not entirely eliminated. To do this, you need to determine what works for each of you individually and then craft a shared strategy that meets both your financial goals and relationship needs.

5.1. Understanding Debt Together

It's imperative to lay out and understand the full picture of your debts. This includes the amount, interest rates, and the timeline for payments for all individual and joint debts. Start by gathering all financial documents related to your debt, including loans, credit card statements, car leases, and other lines of credit. It's important to be open and honest about all outstanding debts. This meticulous record-keeping will serve as the backbone of your debt management strategy.

If this task seems daunting, consider involving a trusted financial advisor to help organize your debt and devise a repayment strategy.

5.2. Debt Repayment Approach

Once you gain clarity on your combined debts, the next step is to choose a repayment strategy. Consider the "snowball" method, where you focus on paying off the smallest debt first, while maintaining minimum payments on larger debts, to create momentum. Alternatively, the "avalanche" method, where you tackle the highest interest debt first, could save you more money over time. Each couple must decide which approach works best for their situation.

In addition, check for any opportunities to refinance or consolidate your debts. With lower interest rates, you could potentially save money and simplify your repayment process.

5.3. Budgeting Basics: A Tool for Tackling Debts

Crafting a budget is fundamental when dealing with debt. Your budget clarifies where your money is going and pinpoints where cost-cutting is possible. Construct your budget around fixed expenses (rent, bills), variable expenses (groceries, leisure), as well as your debt repayments. Be realistic, thorough, and include a contingency allowance for unexpected costs.

Adopt smart spending habits that curb indiscriminate purchases. This can be as simple as planning meals to reduce wastage or choosing home entertainment over expensive nights out. Stick to your budget, but reassure each other that it can be adjusted as necessary.

5.4. Communication: The Heart of Debt Management

The importance of open and ongoing communication cannot be overstated. Prioritizing regular financial discussions can prevent any surprises, mistrust, or resentment related to money matters from cropping up.

Set clear expectations about your shared financial responsibilities.

Define who will be responsible for which aspects of managing the debt, and ensure that both parties are comfortable with the arrangement. Being transparent and honest will alleviate much of the stress and can even pave the way to more collaboration in tackling your combined debt.

Also, acknowledge that paying off debt can take time, so it's okay if your progress seems slower than expected. Encourage each other and celebrate your victories, no matter how small. This positive reinforcement can yield additional motivation to maintain your efforts.

5.5. Emergency Fund: A Safety Net Worth Building

While your primary focus may be debt elimination, setting up an emergency fund is crucial. An emergency fund acts as a shock absorber against unexpected life events such as job loss or sudden illness, preventing you from falling into fresh debt.

Start small. Even a small amount set aside each month can accumulate into a substantial safety net over time. It's advisable to aim for three to six months of living expenses stored in your emergency fund, but remember that your first goal is simply to start saving.

5.6. Addressing the Emotional Side of Debt

Finally, don't lose sight of the fact that dealing with debt is as much emotional as it is financial. The process can stir up all sorts of feelings, from guilt and stress to hopelessness. Yet, facing these emotions openly and together can lead to deeper understanding and stronger support.

Take the time to empathize with your partner's worries, offering comfort and sharing your own anxieties. Remember, the goal here is to fight the debt, not each other. Encourage one another, maintain a supportive environment, and celebrate your wins, no matter how seemingly insignificant they may be.

Indeed, debt can be a daunting challenge, but it can also be a profound opportunity. The journey towards becoming debt-free can deepen your relationship, build mutual respect, and strengthen your shared vision for the future. And once you embrace the right strategies, skills, and mindset, you'll soon discover that the road to financial freedom is definitely a journey worth embarking on together.

Chapter 6. Saving Together: Strategies for Future Security

Starting a savings plan with your partner can feel overwhelming, daunting even, but remember this is a commitment towards shared future prosperity. When couples save together, they not only secure their financial future but also strengthen their bond.

6.1. Understanding the Importance of Joint Savings

Understanding the importance of saving together is the first step in this joint venture. Financial independence is everybody's goal, but achieving it requires planning, dedication, strategic saving and more importantly, teamwork between you and your partner.

Saving together can help cover unexpected expenses, provide a safety net for sudden job loss, fund vacations, build a nest egg for retirement, or finance big-ticket items like a home renovation or a new car. Joint savings can also be the stepping stone for investments that yield higher returns.

6.2. Setting Joint Financial Goals

Setting financial goals is an essential aspect of effective money management. Begin by discussing your long and short-term financial targets. These can range from buying a house or car, planning a dream vacation, saving for children's education, or gearing up for retirement.

In the process, consider each other's perspective, factor in individual aspirations, and respect each other's financial comfort zones. It's crucial that the goals you set are agreed upon and shared, to encourage both parties to work towards them diligently.

For short-term goals, consider saving in a high-yield savings account, while for long-term objectives, investing in retirement accounts, or bonds could be beneficial.

6.3. Creating a Joint Budget

After having set your shared financial targets, the next step is to draft a joint budget. This blueprint should detail your combined income, fixed expenses such as rent or mortgage, utilities, groceries, and bills, as well as discretionary spending like dining out, streaming services, gym memberships etc. It should also earmark funds for your joint savings.

Include a discussion about personal spending limits to maintain transparency and avoid overspending. A budgeting app or software can simplify this process, providing real-time updates and expense tracking.

6.4. Developing a Savings Plan

The key to building savings is consistency, so create a plan that automatically diverts a set percentage of your income to your savings account. Automating the process circumvents the temptation to spend. Also, consider the 'pay yourself first' principle, which involves setting aside a part of your income for savings before budgeting for other expenses.

Each partner should have an equal say in setting the saving rate. As a thumb rule, aim to save 10%-20% of your income. However, this can vary based on your combined income and financial objectives. When salaries increase, consider raising your savings rate correspondingly.

6.5. Contingency Plans and Emergency Funds

Unforeseen expenses can throw a wrench in your financial goals. Therefore, build an emergency fund that has around three to six months' worth of living expenses.

In addition, review and update your insurance plans for health, home, auto, and life coverage. Adequate insurance coverage can help manage risks and shield your savings from unexpected expenses.

6.6. Regular Savings Review

Hold bi-monthly or quarterly 'money dates' to review your budget, savings, and financial goal progress. This will not only keep you both on the same page but also allow for timely adjustments. If you find your savings lagging behind, find areas in your budget to cut back on.

Savings can act as a buffer in life's unpredicted downfalls and set the stage for joint ventures. Be patient. It's essential to remember that saving is a journey, not a sprint. Celebrate small triumphs to keep the motivation high and continuously reassess and adjust your goals and plans as required.

In conclusion, your combined financial security is not something that can be achieved overnight, nor is it something to be left to chance. With careful planning, transparent communication, and dedicated savings, a stable, financially secure future can become your shared reality. Always remember: finance is not just about money, but about securing a future infused with choice, freedom, and peace of mind.

Chapter 7. Dating and Dinero: Discussing Finances Early in a Relationship

The adage, 'Money is the root of all evil,' stems from the fact that money has been at the center of many disputes, disagreements, and breakups in relationships. Hence, a frank conversation about finances is crucial at the initial stages of a relationship, setting a financial foundation for a strong and healthy partnership. This chapter will guide you through these complicated financial discussions, paving your way to a balanced and flourishing relationship.

7.1. The Importance of Early Financial Conversations

Discussing finances early in a relationship may not seem like the most romantic conversation you could have. After all, aren't talks of love, aspirations, and shared interests more alluring? However, sidestepping financial talks can sow seeds of friction that can sprout later into full-blown disputes. Hence, early discussions about money can prevent potential conflicts and ensure financial compatibility. A transparent financial dialogue can reflect shared values, discipline, and commitment to future goals.

7.2. How to Bring Up the Money Topic

Irrespective of the stage of the relationship, the topic of money can be a sensitive issue. Understanding how to bring up this topic can make these conversations less intimidating.

One way to do so is to wait for a 'money moment'—a situation that naturally prompts a financial discussion, such as splitting a bill or planning a trip together. Another approach is to gradually introduce money topics during daily interactions. Observations about economic news, financial goals, or personal buying habits can segue into larger discussions about money.

Remember, patience and gentleness are crucial. The dialogue should be open and non-judgmental to allow both parties to express their financial thoughts, habits, and fears comfortably.

7.3. Understanding Each Other's Money Personalities

Like our personalities, we all have unique money personalities formed through our upbringing, life experiences, and personal attitudes. These can range from being a spender or a saver, or being risk-averse or risk-tolerant.

Understanding each other's money personalities is essential. This comprehension can help you predict how your partner might react to financial situations like lifestyle adjustments, unexpected expenses, or investment opportunities. Further, it can reveal compatibility and potential areas of financial conflict.

7.4. Setting Financial Boundaries

Setting clear financial boundaries is integral to maintaining harmony. You and your partner may have different views on what constitutes as necessities and splurges, how much debt is acceptable, or how income should be allocated. Such discrepancies can cause friction unless clear boundaries are set.

Highlight mutual agreement on aspects like how you'll split bills, the obligation process in case of common purchases, and limitations concerning debt should be discussed. Establishing these guidelines earlier within the dating lifespan can prevent financial misunderstandings and provide a roadmap for handling finances as the relationship grows.

7.5. Transparency and Trust-building

Transparent about past financial missteps and current financial standing, such as debts, loans, savings, and investments, builds trust in a relationship. This openness can enable both parties to work together to overcome financial hardships and align their efforts towards common financial goals.

Sharing credit reports or bank statements could be a step in this direction but remember, this should be a reciprocal and voluntary act. It is not about 'checking' on each other's finances, but creating an environment of financial honesty and accountability.

7.6. Planning for the Future

Discussions about future financial goals, be it big-ticket purchases, starting a family, early retirement, or travel plans, can provide insight into each other's financial values and expectations. It can kickstart proactive financial planning and help align financial habits and contributions towards these shared goals. These talks should encompass savings strategies, investment plans, emergency funds and timeframe to achieve these financial targets.

7.7. Financial Literacy

Building a common understanding about financial concepts and principles fosters better financial decision-making. Understanding concepts like interest rates, investment risks, benefits of savings, tax planning, and insurance are beneficial. This knowledge can ensure that both parties can contribute constructively in financial discussions and jointly manage finances with confidence.

In conclusion, when you start dating, financial conversations seem daunting and awkward. But acknowledging and planning for financial issues early can lead to financial harmony in a relationship. It forms a financial bedrock that not only enhances understanding and trust but brings you closer to your shared aspirations. Remember, money talks aren't about the dollars and cents; it's about values, compatibility, dreams, and your shared future. Therefore, learn to nimbly navigate these tricky conversations— after all, love, trust and finances are the three pillars that hold a relationship sturdy.

Chapter 8. Managing Money During Marriage Transitions

Marriage transitions can be monumental moments in your life, which also signify significant financial changes. We span the range from the joy of saying "I do" to the heart-wrenching decision of parting ways, taking in the journey of parenthood along the way. Here, we explore guiding principles to help manage the financial implications of these life-altering events, thereby fostering financial stability and wellness in your relationship.

8.1. The Beginning: Merging Finances After Marriage

Once the honeymoon period ends, reality descends with its pile of practicalities. One such practical aspect is merging finances as a couple. So, how do you begin?

Discuss financial goals early on. Clear communication is crucial in maintaining financial harmony. Both partners should discuss their short-term and long-term financial goals. It could range from buying a home, saving for a vacation, or preparing for retirement. Align your financial objectives and establish a mutual understanding of your financial responsibilities.

Establish a budget. Start by understanding each other's spending habits and accommodate them in the budget. Determine your combined monthly income, fixed expenses, discretionary spending, and savings. Deciding who pays for what and how much each contributes proportionately can be beneficial. Save receipts, track expenses, and evaluate your budget regularly to keep it realistic and flexible.

Practically deal with bank accounts. One size doesn't fit all! Some couples prefer separate bank accounts, some opt for a joint account, while others choose to have both. Discuss and choose what suits you the best.

8.2. Parenthood and Planning for the Future

Becoming a parent is a transformative, joyous event. However, it also includes financial adjustments.

Analyze your insurance policies. With the arrival of a child, it becomes crucial to reconsider your insurance coverage. Make sure to include your child in your health care provisions and think about life insurance policies and their beneficiaries. A will or trust might also be beneficial.

Plan for Estate. Estate planning is crucial when you've children. Having a will, deciding on guardianships or setting up a trust fund, it ensures your child's future security if something unfavorable happens.

Education funding. Once a family starts to grow, college funding becomes a vital aspect of financial planning. Different countries have different systems like the 529 plan in the US, which allows tax-free savings for future school costs.

8.3. Surviving the Storm: Handling Finances During Divorce

Sometimes, unfortunately, marriages end in divorce, bringing with it financial fallout. Here's how to navigate this tricky terrain.

Understand your assets and liabilities. Ascertain the value of all your shared and individual assets and liabilities. This could include anything from your house, car, savings, stocks, credit card debt to loans.

Get Professional Help. Hire a financial advisor if possible. They can help you review your financial health, assisting in understanding ramifications of asset splits and offering guidance for future financial well-being.

Protect your credit. Credit scores are crucial in determining your financial security. In the process of untangling finances, ensure your joint accounts are paid off or frozen. Monitor your credit score regularly.

Separate liabilities. In the split, make sure all individual debts are in the appropriate person's names. Joint debts can impact both parties' credit scores.

8.4. Later Life: Managing Finances in Retirement

The golden years offer opportunities for relaxation and exploration but can also come with financial concerns. Here is how to ensure a financially secure retirement.

Plan ahead. Retirement planning should be initiated early on in your marriage. Regularly contribute to retirement funds and consider hiring a financial advisor.

Invest in diverse income streams. Annuity payments, rental income, dividends, part-time work or royalties, having different income streams can help deal with unexpected expenses.

Consider living situation. Downsizing and moving to a more affordable area or living community can substantially lower your cost of living during retirement.

Understanding Long-Term Care. As aging progresses, long-term care becomes a significant consideration. Look into long-term care insurance and become familiar with Medicare/Medicaid provisions in your country.

Navigating financial matters during marriage transitions can be a complex endeavor. However, with open and honest communication, informed decision-making, and proactive planning, it can very well be an opportunity to jointly navigate towards a secure financial future. Each transition in itself is a learning, holding lessons that contribute towards building a money-wise, mutually supportive relationship. Embrace these periods of transition with courage, patience, and empathy.

With these tools and strategies at your disposal, rest assured that you are well-equipped to manage your finances during every stage of your marriage, ensuring lasting financial harmony.

Chapter 9. Joint Investments: Opportunities and Considerations

Managing finances as a couple presents a whole range of opportunities, challenges, and decisions that need to be taken, one of which is making joint investments. Done right, these can significantly contribute to your mutual financial goals and day-to-day economic security. However, ensuring you make sound decisions requires thorough understanding of the investment landscape, your shared financial status, goals, risk tolerance, as well as effective communication. Let's embark on this comprehensive exploration of joint investments, walking through the doors of opportunities they open and the considerations that they demand.

9.1. Understanding Joint Investments

When you invest as a couple, the assets you acquire or the ventures you engage in are owned by both of you. It could be property, stocks, bonds, mutual funds or even a business venture. The ownership status matters because it impacts tax liabilities, decision-making powers, risks, and even outcomes upon death or separation.

It's important to engage in a thoughtful consideration of your individual and joint financial realities and goals. This lays a solid foundation for making informed decisions about the types of investments you should pursue, the amount to invest, and the risk you're willing and able to take. It also forms a basis for open discussions about how to deal with potential disagreements or unforeseen circumstances.

9.2. Advantages of Joint Investments

There are several reasons why you might consider making joint investments:

1. Income pooling: Larger initial capital can enable you to invest in opportunities that might have been unattainable individually.

2. Risk spreading: Sharing the financial risk can make an investment less daunting.

3. Shared decision-making: Two heads can be better than one; different perspectives can provide a more balanced view.

4. Learning together: The process of researching and monitoring investments can be a great opportunity to learn about finance.

5. Strengthening the relationship: Shared goals and endeavors can bring you closer, and the progress made can be rewarding and satisfying.

9.3. Types of Joint Investments

While several investment avenues can be explored jointly, some common ones include:

1. Real estate: Buying a property together can be a source of shared income if you decide to rent it out, or it could become a home that you share.

2. Stocks and bonds: If you both are interested in the stock market, you could pool your resources to purchase shares.

3. Mutual funds: These allow you to invest money in a diversified portfolio of stocks, bonds, etc. with the advantage of professional management.

4. Joint bank accounts: Though not strictly an investment, such an account can earn interest and serve as a base for further joint

investments.

5. Business ventures: If you share a business idea, you could consider partnering.

Each of these investment types presents different opportunities and risks, requires distinct considerations, and suits different financial contexts and goals.

9.4. Considerations before embarking on Joint Investments

While joint investments present exciting opportunities, they also call for careful consideration. It's not a decision to make impulsively, and there are aspects you have to take into account:

1. Financial Goals: Ensure you share and understand each other's financial goals. This forms the basis for deciding what and how much to invest.

2. Risk Tolerance: A shared understanding of each other's risk tolerance can help prevent disagreements in the future.

3. Ownership Structure: The decision of ownership structure—whether joint tenancy, tenants in common, or community property—depends on your marital status, retirement plans, etc.

4. Legal Aspects: Consider the legal implications of joint ownership, which may need legal advice.

5. Contingency Planning: Discuss scenarios like separation, death, or one partner wanting to exit the investment.

9.5. Navigating Differences

Differences in opinion and approach are inevitable. However, they need not be roadblocks. Proper communication, respect for each other's views, and negotiation strategies can help you find common ground and move forward. Remember, financial decisions are never just about money—they're about your dreams, ambitions, insecurities, and your shared future.

To wrap up, joint investments offer couples a pathway to realizing their mutual financial dreams, provided they're approached with mutual understanding, clarity of communication, and thorough awareness. Not only are they a financial venture, they're also an enriching journey of learning, shared experiences, and relationship-building. Begin your investment journey with eyes wide open, filled with understanding, and a shared vision for what you want your future to look like.

Chapter 10. Financial Transparency: Cultivating Trust and Accountability

Open communication is the foundation of trust, particularly when it comes to finances. This can't be more emphasized in the context of relationships where financial transparency is critical in fostering not just trust, but also accountability. In this piece, we delve into the different aspects of financial transparency, how to cultivate it, and its implications for relationship longevity.

10.1. Understanding Financial Transparency

As the term indicates, financial transparency in relationships is about openness regarding money matters. It involves being honest and forthright about income, savings, spending habits, financial goals, debts, and more. It's crucial, especially when your decisions might directly affect your partner.

10.2. Why Transparency is Key

Financial transparency is vital for several reasons:

1. Eases Anxiety: Knowing your partner's financial standing can ease anxiety about the future and create a stronger sense of stability.

2. Enhances Trust: Regular discussions about finances can enhance mutual trust and respect.

3. Prevents Surprises: Transparency helps you avoid nasty surprises like undisclosed debts and bad credit.

4. Promotes Financial Health: Open discussions about money can educate each other about financial management, leading to better financial decisions.

10.3. Cultivating Transparency

Cultivating financial transparency consists of three major steps:

1. Open the Dialogue: Begin the conversation about financial matters. Choose a calm, comfortable environment to minimize stress.

2. Share Information: Provide each other with complete information about your income, savings, investments, loans, credit health, and financial goals.

3. Discuss Expectations: Talk about your spending habits, investment choices, saving strategies and short and long-term financial goals. Ensure you're on the same page.

10.4. Handling Reservations

Even with the importance of financial transparency widely acknowledged, there can be hesitations. These could stem from:

1. Personal: Previous experiences such as financial trauma, or spending discrepancies could create resistance.

2. Cultural: Some cultures regard money discussions as a taboo, which can be another barrier.

3. Gender Stereotypes: Traditional gender roles can lead to unnecessary pressure on one partner or miscommunications about financial roles in the home.

For every problem listed above, the best and probably the only solution is open, non-judgmental conversation. Create a safe space where both partners can openly discuss any worries, fears, or concerns about finances and the prospect of sharing this information completely.

10.5. Making Transparency Practice

Making the practice of financial transparency a norm requires commitment and patience. Here's a step-by-step guide:

1. Schedule Regular Finance Dates: Keep aside regular, non-negotiable time for money talks. This keeps you updated.

2. Use Tools: Budget tracking apps, financial spreadsheets, joint bank accounts, are good ways to keep payments and saving targets transparent.

3. Share Management: Whether it's paying bills or making investments, share the responsibilities. This leads to equal ownership in financial matters.

4. Seek Professional Help: If discussions repeatedly lead to disagreements, consider seeking advice from a financial coach or relationship counselor.

10.6. Accountability: The Companion to Transparency

Being transparent about finances does not solely suffices; it requires being held accountable for the shared financial goals and commitments.

Accountability ensures financial tasks undertake completion timely, budgets are adhered to, and saving targets reached. Here are few basics to practice:

1. Set Clear Financial Boundaries and Goals: Both partners should agree on specific spending limits, saving goals, and investment

plans.

2. Assign Responsibilities: Divide financial roles and responsibilities. Ensure both partners equally share the financial management.

3. Monitor Goals: Regular reviews of your progress towards the shared financial goals. Adjust the goals as necessary to align with any new changes in your financial situation.

4. Encourage and Support: Appreciate your partner's efforts in sticking to the commitments, and support them in hardships. Encouragement boosts morale and nurtures the faith in shared goals.

10.7. Ahead-Looking

Financial transparency is not a phase or a one-off process, but a journey. It is important to evolve the approach with changing circumstances, and continue to maintain openness about every financial aspect.

Change can be challenging, but the rewards of a financially harmonious relationship make the journey worthwhile. Remember, the key to fostering financial transparency lies in open communication, understanding, trust, and accountability.

By cultivating financial transparency, you are not just fostering a healthy relationship with your partner, but also paving the path for personal financial growth and maturity. This is indeed a journey worthwhile, not just for your relationship, but also for your individual growth.

Keep going, keep growing, and remember - open conversations are the key to financial transparency.

Chapter 11. Turning Financial Difficulties into Growth Opportunities

Understanding that financial difficulties aren't merely roadblocks but potential stepping stones towards a healthier financial life is crucial. Ups and downs are a part of every journey, including the financial one. Visualizing these hurdles not as setbacks, but as catalysts for growth encourages a positive mindset and proactivity.

11.1. Recognizing financial struggles

Before unraveling the road to growth, acknowledging that a problem exists is vital. Often, monetary complications lurk beneath the surface of spending habits, unseen or disregarded until they erupt into a full-scale financial crisis. We advise a proactive approach, identifying signs of financial difficulty promptly, before it swells into an unmanageable situation.

Financial struggles manifest in various forms, such as consistent overspending, rising debts, or inadequate savings. Each of these signs reflects an inherent issue - complacency towards money. We'll subsequently dive deeper into the intricacies of these signs, providing you with the necessary insights and tools to identify financial vulnerabilities.

1. Consistent Overspending: A common symptom of deep-seated financial difficulty is chronic overspending. If your monthly expenses consistently exceed your income, it's high time for a financial check-up. Remember, habitual overspending is analogous to a fast-moving vehicle without brakes – both dangerous and unsustainable.

2. Rising Debts: If you're continuously relying on credit cards or loans to finance your lifestyle, it signifies monetary instability. Rising debts often stem from reckless financial behavior and are an undeniable sign that you're living beyond your means.

3. Inadequate Savings: The absence of a financial cushion in the form of savings or investments is another red flag. Savings provide a safety net during contingencies, and lack thereof can push you into a vicious debt circle – a situation best avoided.

11.2. Embracing a growth mindset

The biggest deterrent to financial growth isn't necessarily lack of funds, but rather the absence of a growth mindset. Viewing financial struggles as lessons learned and opportunities for enhancement rather than mere setbacks is pivotal in cultivating mental fortitude.

To adopt a growth mindset, completely restructuring your perspective is required. Consider every financial misstep as a feedback mechanism instead of declaring it a failure. For instance, if inability to save effectively is an issue you're grappling with, view it as an opportunity to study various saving strategies and align them with your needs.

11.3. Developing a financial recovery plan

Upon identification of financial struggles and cultivating a growth mindset, the next step is to instigate a recovery plan. A recovery plan acts as a roadmap, directing you towards your financial goals while keeping your actions in check.

1. Budget: Nothing shouts financial recovery louder than a well-strategized budget. A budget serves as a navigational tool, guiding you through your income, expenses, savings, and investments.

2. Debt Reduction Plan: High-interest debts act as kryptonite to financial growth. A sound debt reduction plan helps tackle your loans methodically, starting either from the smallest debt or the one with the highest interest depending upon the strategy you follow.

3. Emergency Fund: The role of an emergency fund in mitigating financial risks can't be overstated. Aim to accumulate three to six months' worth of living expenses as a part of this fund.

11.4. Communication - The key to aligning financial goals

Open and honest communication forms the basis of joint financial management. It's essential to discuss financial situations, ambitions, and fears openly. This gives both parties a clear understanding of where they stand and what needs to be achieved together.

Create a safe environment for these discussions. Never resort to blame games or finger-pointing. Instead, aim for constructive conversation that can lead to better financial understanding and planning.

11.5. Utilizing professional help

Sometimes, the complexity of financial problems can be overwhelming. In such situations, professional help, like a financial advisor, can provide a fresh, educated perspective and propose effective remedies. These professionals have the experience, skills, and tools to tailor strategies that fit your unique financial situation, turning potential failures into opportunities.

In conclusion, remember, financial struggles are not the end of the world, but rather, signposts indicating the need for changes in behaviors and habits. Once these signs are recognized and necessary steps to rectify them are taken, anyone can navigate the turbulent waters of financial difficulties towards solid ground. Utilizing these challenges as a springboard to achieve financial wellness can transform your relationship with money, creating harmony and understanding in your personal relationships as well.

And as you embark on this journey, remember the four key pillars – recognition, mindset, planning, and communication. With these, there's no financial difficulty that you can't convert into a growth opportunity.